Action Karate Quilts

First published by AuthorHouse 10/28/05

ISBN: 1-4208-8621-5 (sc)

Printed in the United States of America
Bloomington, Indiana

This book is printed on acid-free paper.

authorHOUSE

1663 LIBERTY DRIVE
BLOOMINGTON, INDIANA 47403
(800) 839-8640
www.authorhouse.com

Contents

Dedication

*T*o my husband Michael, our son Zachary, and our daughter Jessica, thanks for the endless and loving support.

To my mother and father Marie and August "Gus" Kolbe for unknowingly sparking my interest in quilting by giving me the *Reader's Digest Crafts & Hobbies* book, after I graduated from college. They knew I had a deep down interest in "making things".

To John McCray, the Sensei of the American Martial Arts Academy in Cape May County, New Jersey, for great self defense instructions.

And to the Mayo Clinic in Rochester, Minnesota, especially neurosurgeon Dr. Fredrick Meyer and neurologist Dr. Gregory D. Cascino, I thank you for giving me another chance.

I gratefully acknowledge…

The South Shore Stitchers Quilting Guild in Southern New Jersey and the South Shore Stitchers members who precision pieced some of the HEAD patterns to be used as pictures in the book. I gratefully thank:

Faye Wasleski
Donna Soffe
Nancy Byers

Phyllis Marshall I was just bursting with ideas to share with others. All you had to do was ask. Thank you Phyllis for asking and for being patient. Keep on stitching. It's good for the brain.

The individuals involved in the various forms of martial arts whose faces were used as examples of photo transfer for appliqué. You make the martial arts look like fun:

Dr. Lou Demoulin,
Carol Vermeil
Dexter McCleon.

John Scarpa for a photograph which I was able to use part of in a quilt.

Carolyn Kolbe for the photograph of her sister the author.

The C-THRU RULER Co. for E-mailing me a photocopy of their Proportional Scale. It is a tool that I love to use in order to size a photo accurately for a perfect fit in a pattern.

Minx Boren for editing.

Christine Solazzi for her computer expertise from Kube Quest Graphic Designs, Inc.

Introduction

People who do not like to create and sew by hand, by machine or both, see it all as work. But for those who love fabric art, it can be a soothing and healing experience filled with the joy of knowing you are creating something from within yourself. The wonder of seeing what can come out of creative self expression is amazing. Bringing designs alive is thrilling. I love to keep busy doing all the different parts of a project, from making a design to getting fabric, piecing or appliquéing, quilting and finally finding a home for my creation. After graduating college I took a job in Hotel & Restaurant Management. But always an artist by heart, I discovered quilting as a hobby. It all began, with a *Reader's Digest Craft & Hobbies* book printed in 1979. I have been hooked or, I should say, pinned ever since.

Karate has been around for hundreds of years. When my son Zack was 5 years old, he began studying karate at the American Martial Arts Academy led by John McCray. Coming from a small town, it was an opportunity for Zack to get out and socialize in an organized sport activity. As he obtained each new color belt, he also built strong muscles in a healthy, friendly environment. Next, my daughter Jessica joined in. Years later, even I took it up after watching many of their classes and observing their strength and flexibility improve. In the classes, repetition of the movements was used to train students to react quickly and precisely, so that if needed, the correct protective movement would come instantly and instinctively. The training gave us a sense of security while also increasing our awareness of our surroundings.

The original karate pattern quilt, called "American Martial Arts Quilt", was a gift I made for my son, when he earned his senior black belt using a flag motif to symbolize the name of the school. The quilt depicts the diversity of the school's members of all ages, genders, and ethnic backgrounds. The belt colors progress from the beginning, which is white, to the end, which is black, with three additional master stars. That quilt won an Honorable Mention Award from the National Arts Program (NAP) in 2004 for Cape May County, New Jersey. My daughter also earned her junior black belt, which is the equivalent to her brother's senior black belt without the training with weapons.

Eventually I had to stop taking karate because of a neurological problem that was causing seizures that could not be controlled with medication. The surgical route to treat my problem had to be faced. I could not drive a car until the problem was resolved, but I could still quilt. I even brought my sewing machine to the Mayo Clinic in Rochester to keep me busy and positively focused with an incentive to keep going. I was determined to finish my current project while at the same time being inspired to do more. The staff commented that they had seen a lot of people bring activities to the hospital to keep them busy but I was the first to bring a sewing machine and an iron. They restricted my ironing for fear that I would hurt myself, so my husband, Mike volunteered to help me out with that (probably the only time he will willingly iron in his life).

*A*fter successfully recovering from the operation I felt as if I had another chance at life. I pursued my passion and joined a quilting guild. At the South Shore Stitchers Quilting Guild meeting, I met people like myself who love making quilts. After showing them the karate quilt that I had made, some women asked where I had gotten the pattern. I explained that I had made it myself. Seeing the interest in it, I have decided to share the instructions for making quilts with a karate theme with others.

My original karate quilt used heads that were designed into the pattern. That pattern did not allow you to choose a variety of faces and positions. It was a take it or leave it design. I thought that people might like to be able to choose their own HEAD and BLOCK patterns, so I designed a square/diamond head method. Therefore, you select the style of HEAD and use it in any of the applicable BLOCKS. (If necessary, the BLOCK patterns will say which HEAD patterns are applicable to them.) You may also select which direction you would prefer the BLOCK figures to face, left or right, by choosing the tracing method. Therefore, there are many opportunities for creative interpretation.

M y original "American Arts Quilt", 1996

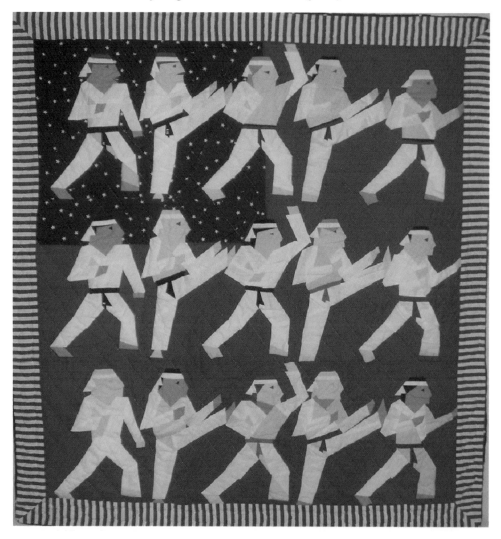

Quilt Gallery

 Examples #1, #2, #3

1. Action Karate Sampler / 2 joined BLOCKS Pieced pattern example using pieced HEADS
   The male figure on the left is made from BLOCK # 1 with HEAD #13
   The female figure on the right is made from BLOCK # 6 and HEAD # 3
2. Appliquéd body and photo transferred head example of kick boxers.
3. Pieced pattern using a photo transfer for the HEAD

(2)
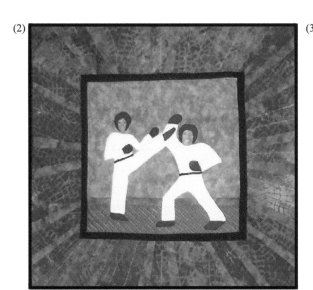

(3)

(1)

Using the Book to Piece Your Action Karate Sampler

 *T*o begin, you must understand the wording and symbols used in the instructions.

When the word "block" without capital letters is used in the name of a BLOCK (shown with capital letters), it is in reference to a defensive body position used in martial arts. BLOCK in all capital letters refers to the precision piecing BLOCK pattern. Each BLOCK has a pattern number "#".

A BLOCK is made by precisely putting Pieces together to make Sections, and putting Sections together to make a BLOCK. In other words:

Pieces (marked with assembly order and fabric identification code) combine into

Sections (defined by dotted lines within a pattern and your colored markings) which
combine to make each

BLOCK

HEADS are similar in their structure to BLOCKS, as Pieces make Sections, and Sections make HEADS. The completed HEADS are then treated as a Piece within a Section, then used to make a BLOCK.

The faces on these patterns use very small pieces. HEADS # 1 & 2 & 3 & 4 are the simplest, as they consist of a single Section. Using the reverse foundation piecing method makes piecing possible and rewarding but tedious when dealing with very small pieces. Of course you may enlarge the patterns as much as you like which would make them easier to work with.

Be generous with the seam allowance for the HEAD piece to facilitate adding it to the rest of the pattern.

Note: When assembling the BLOCK, if it says to "join", it means only the immediate Sections being worked on. The directions given for making BLOCKS and HEADS are simplified, for example in BLOCK #6, it says "piece Sections 1 & 2 & 3 & 4; join". I find it easier to make one Section at a time, make another, then join, then make another and join, and so on. If you make all the little Sections at once, it is very hard to identify them. Do not do the other groups of Sections until specified, as the order of construction is critical.

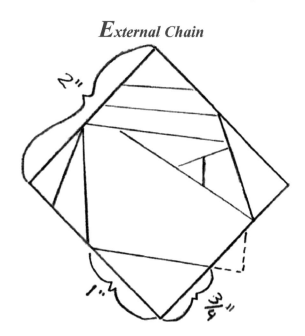 dding the color markings on the freezer paper really helps during the piecing process. Having every clue possible during construction is helpful, because the little pieces are like unidentifiable pieces in a jig saw puzzle. It is helpful to draw in little arrows perpendicular to the dotted lines between pieces that will be joined together. To help you line them up exactly when two pieces are [facing each other] and therefore the patterns can not be seen, put a pin through one arrow then flip to the other side, making sure it lines up exactly with the arrow on the other side.

The squiggly line shown, represents areas in the design, where quilting there, would add details to the pattern, such as the arm and belt area.

*E*xternal Chain   *I*nternal Chin

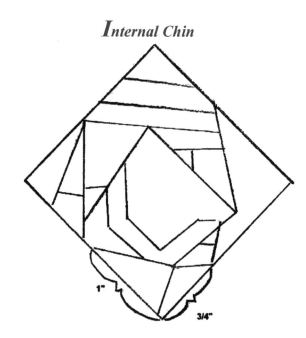

- Remember that if you enlarge the pattern 200%, the distance up from the chin will be 1 1/2 ", and to the back of the neck will be 2".

Also remember that after sewing, the patterns may not look perfect from the back, but when turned over to the fabric side, they look great. The pattern is somewhat forgiving though it is called precision piecing.

•Note: Do not make patterns with buttons for very young children as they may be dangerous.

How to use the Book for Applique and Photo Heads

Perhaps you want to consider using a photo on fabric of your selected karate student or teacher (sensei) and appliquéing it onto the BLOCK. In that case I would recommend using the background color fabric in the HEAD area of the BLOCK, and then apply the photo onto that. See Example #2. If you are fully into appliqué, you could use the whole body pattern for that. Cut out the whole body and use as a template to make your appliqué piece. You may want to trim the edges of the pattern to make them smoother and less rigid. Don't forget to add a seam allowance to the pattern.

When substituting a photo for a pieced HEAD, you need to take your photo and photo copy it to the correct size and direction you want it to end up facing on your BLOCK. This can be tedious, but be patient as the results can be very satisfying. In most cases you will find a proportion tool to be very helpful. It will enable you to easily figure what percentage in size (decrease or increase) that the photo needs to be in order to fit the pattern.

As in Example #3, to match the background fabric of the BLOCK with the HEAD background, cut out the face of your karate figure and tape it onto the HEAD diamond shaped fabric (the size of the HEAD plus the seam allowance). Tape some uniform fabric under the face in the appropriate place. Try out your HEAD by placing it under the dull side of the freezer paper and looking through. If it's correct, copy it onto the transfer fabric you choose.

The colors do not always print out exactly the same as the original fabric, so you may have to fiddle with the tones on your printer to make it as close as you like.

You will also find that the head in a photo will generally appear to be smaller than the pieced HEAD patterns. See Example #3.

I have tried different photo transfer methods and products. They all can work, but may have limits. Remember that some of them are not water safe and all of the work you do may be suddenly washed away. I have tried spraying water repellant on some of these products as well as on regular cotton fabric ironed onto freezer paper (to help it get through the printer) as an experiment and it seems to be working, though I am not sure how long it will last. Instead, to be safe I would reapply some repellant after every wash and only choose this type of transfer on items that do not need to be washed frequently, like wall hangings).

*T*he Quick Fuse Inkjet Fabric sheets are good for the appliqué method though their texture is a little thick and stiff. Also, be very careful when washing as I have ruined some that I mistakenly put in the dryer under heat.

Remember when photocopying that you may need to do the 100% mirror setting on the copier. Looking at the freezer paper drawing, what you are seeing is the opposite of the way your BLOCK and HEAD will be facing. Look through the glossy side of the freezer paper to see the correct direction.

Getting to Work

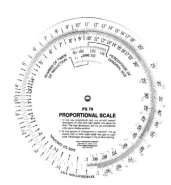

$\blacklozenge$ **T**ools / Tracing the Pattern/ Fabric Selection / Quantity Needed / Marking the Pattern with Fabric Code

TOOLS

1. Sewing machine
2. Quilter's fabric cutting board
3. See-through ruler or measuring tool
4. Rotating cutter
5. Bright light (obtained through a window during daylight, or a light tracing machine)
6. Carbon paper (not necessary if using light tracing method)
7. Poster Board (not necessary if using light tracing method)
8. Scotch Tape or Staples (used to apply carbon paper to poster board)
9. Freezer Paper (the shiny side is the heat activated adhesive side)
10. Pencil, pale colored washable markers, or colored pencils, quilter's markers
11. Scissors
12. Threads, Pins, and Needles for sewing and basting
13. Proportional Scale (used for photo transfers and pattern designing)
14. Iron-on adhesive (for appliqué)
15. Ironing board and an iron

WORK AREA PREPARATION

Pre-wash and iron fabrics before cutting.
Set up the sewing machine on a straight stitch ----, 2.5 length, thread pressure 3. Have an ironing board and iron nearby.
Do not use steam.

TRACING THE PATTERN

After you have selected your patterns and have enlarged them to your desired size, you will need to copy them onto the non-shiny side of freezer paper. There are many ways to trace a pattern; the easiest is using a light tracing machine or a bright window. However, if you do not have one, you may choose one of the carbon paper methods.

The carbon paper methods 1 & 2:

1. Using this method will make the design appear backwards or mirror imaged, though your final BLOCK or HEAD will appear as originally planned as you will be sewing the fabric onto the reverse side of the freezer paper (which is the shiny side). Tape or staple carbon tracing papers, shiny carbon facing up, onto a piece of poster board. The poster board must be at least the size of the final BLOCK. Then lay freezer paper (shiny side up) on top of the carbon paper. Next, lay the design (right side up) on top of the freezer paper, and attach it so that it will not slide while tracing.

2. Using this second method will avoid the mirror image on the freezer paper, though the completed BLOCK will appear backwards when completed. The top layer is the design you are tracing. Below that, place carbon paper (shiny side facing down). Under the carbon paper, place the freezer paper shiny side down.

*H*aving the karate figures being able to face right or left, will be convenient for placing figures in confrontation poses (facing each other). See Example #1.

The BLOCKS in this book are in inches, 7"x 9 1/2", so that they can fit in the book. I would recommend that you photo copy them at least 200%, because of the many small pieces. If you copy them at 200%, your final BLOCK will be 14" x 19". If you copy them at 300% a BLOCK will be 21" x 28 1/2".

The HEADS in the book are 2" square. Enlarged 200% the size will be 4" square. At 300% the size will be 6" square.

Note: If you are enlarging the pattern by scanning into a personal computer, place the HEAD selection onto the BLOCK, and then scan them together as one piece.

Precision piecing becomes easier the more accurately you keep the designs. Make sure to copy the same type of line (dashed or straight), as the dashed lines will indicate where the patterns will be cut apart in sections. You will find when you trace the fabric code and sewing sequence, that they will appear backwards as well. If this is a problem, hold the pattern up to a mirror to read your writing, or try to write backwards when copying the BLOCKS. Making an extra copy of the design you will be doing either on freezer paper or regular paper to use as a reference while you are working will help. The trick to making precision piecing easy is to put in as many clues to help your work along. Remember that once you start cutting up the pieces, it can be a challenge putting them back together.

Shown with 1/4" seam allowance

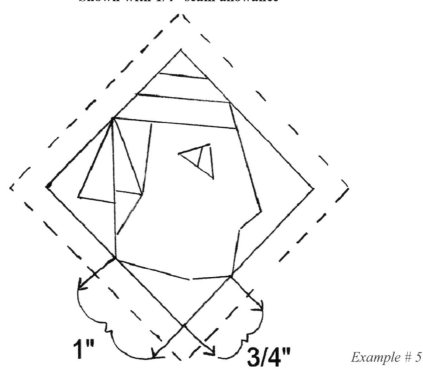

1"

3/4"

Example # 5

Seam Allowance

The patterns do not include the seam allowance. So make sure when you are trimming your BLOCK or HEAD that you include the 1/4". See Example #5 above:

Fabric Selection

The original karate quilt was made using mostly solid colored fabric with different hues or shades to give it a more three dimensional effect. This is not necessary, though I would recommend very small, undefined prints to add texture, but to not distract from the design.

Since there are many small pieces in the BLOCKS, you may be able to use many scraps of fabric for items such as eyes, hair, or mouth. Organize a little fabric sampler of all the fabrics you will be using. Assign a code letter to each fabric, and write it next to the piece of fabric on the sampler as a reference guide. This code letter will also be on each freezer paper foundation for easy identification at the time of piecing. Each piece of the Section is also numbered with its sewing sequence. You may also color the lines of the Sections to help reference them. Mark the outer line of a BLOCK as a solid line, and dot the inner Section lines. You may also want to color in each section a different color, which is where water-soluble markers or colored pencils may help.

In some of the examples shown in the book, different shades of color were used for pieces of the uniform and background. The pattern has been simplified to make these areas one specific fabric color. The fabric quantities given are for an "all one color uniform and background".

Pattern Size

The Pattern Sampler used (see Example #1), consists of an aggressive BLOCK facing a defensive BLOCK, as well as the floor, walls, ceiling, and trim. The suggested fabric requirement for this 2 BLOCK Pattern Example is for patterns expanded 200% from the book size, (which would be 14" x 19", per BLOCK). Follow the same fabric requirement; if you use just one BLOCK expanded 300% from the original size. The BLOCK then would be 21" x 28.5". A 150% increase in a BLOCK size would be 10.5" x 14.5".

Fabric Requirement & Codes

Sample Pattern	Quantity	Color Code
Background fabric	1 yard	A
Floor	1/4 yard (not a fat qtr.)	F
White		
(used for uniforms & whites of eyes)	1/2 yard	U
Skin (head, hands, and feet)	scraps	X
Eye	scraps	E
Belt	scraps	B
Hair	scraps	H
Lips	scraps	L
Side Walls	(2) 23" x 3-1/2" or 1/4 yard	W
Binding	1/4 yard (not a fat qtr.)	M
Ceiling	38" x 2-1/2" or long scrap	C
Backing	38" x 30" (oversized) or 1-1/8 yard	

*T*he Action Karate Sampler Example #1 shows some appliqué pieces and buttons added to it for highlight. These items are not mentioned in the fabric listing.

When a piece in the pattern has a fabric code of A/X, that means the fabric used will depend on whether you chose and internal or external chin HEAD. When a piece has a fabric code of X/H that means that the head may be skin colored "X", or hair colored "H".

When it come to cutting the fabric, check your measuring tools to make sure they are accurate. Then when cutting the fabric bias grain, do not panic, as using the freezer paper as a foundation, stabilizes the fabric. However, be more careful dealing with this on pieces that will be along the edge of the BLOCK, in which case the edges should be cut straight on grain, if possible.

Always begin with Piece 1 in Section 1, of the BLOCK or HEAD. * Note that some HEADS have only one Section. Lay a piece of fabric larger than the area to be covered (including the 1/4" seam allowance), with the back side of the fabric against the shiny side of the freezer paper and press in place. Place the front side and correct edge of the next piece of fabric, facing the correct edge of the appropriate piece attached to the freezer paper, and pin in place along the sewing line. Fold the fabric open and hold it up to a light to if you want to make sure you have enough fabric to cover the piece, including the 1/4" seam allowance. On the outside of BLOCKS and HEADS leave up to 1/2" seam allowance for leeway when trimming, when you get to adding the HEAD to a piece or finally piecing BLOCKS together and adding edges.

*T*urn the pins perpendicular to the seam before stitching. Then, after each line is sewn, trim the seam allowance by folding the freezer paper backwards. It is alright to rip the freezer paper off the fabric where the seam allowances for previous lines cross over the line. Then you will be able to fold the edges to one side before moving onto the next Piece. Fold fabric open and hold up to a light to see what you have done and check your coverage. Next, trim the fabric edge from the seam, 1/4". Fold open the newly sewn-on piece and hold it that way, flipping the pattern paper so that you can iron from the non-adhesive side of the freezer paper. That process will attach the fabric to the paper without having the freezer paper stick to the iron. Move onto the next piece and repeat the process.

Mistakes to Avoid: Do not try to cut the pieces exactly to size before working. It is best to be generous with pieces to be sure you have adequate coverage for when the fabric is opened over the pattern after sewing and pressing in place. You may even want to do a sample stitch using a large stitch length and testing your work before going back over it with the regular stitch length.

Action Karate Sample Pattern

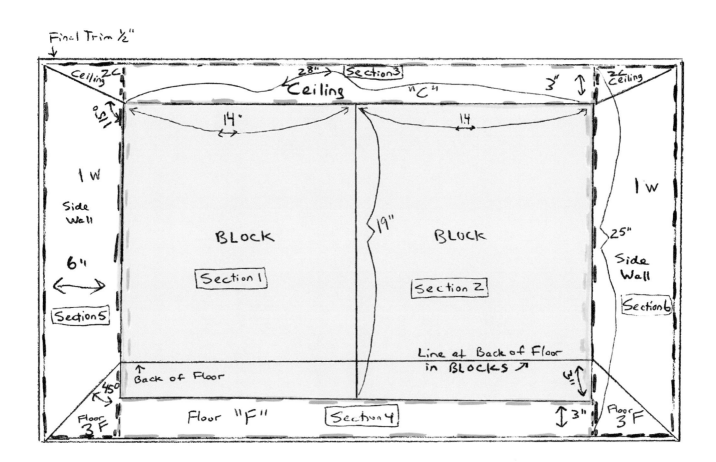

Final Size: 41" w x 26"1

Showing Sections of Example #1

"Action Karate" Sampler Pattern (Not in proportion)

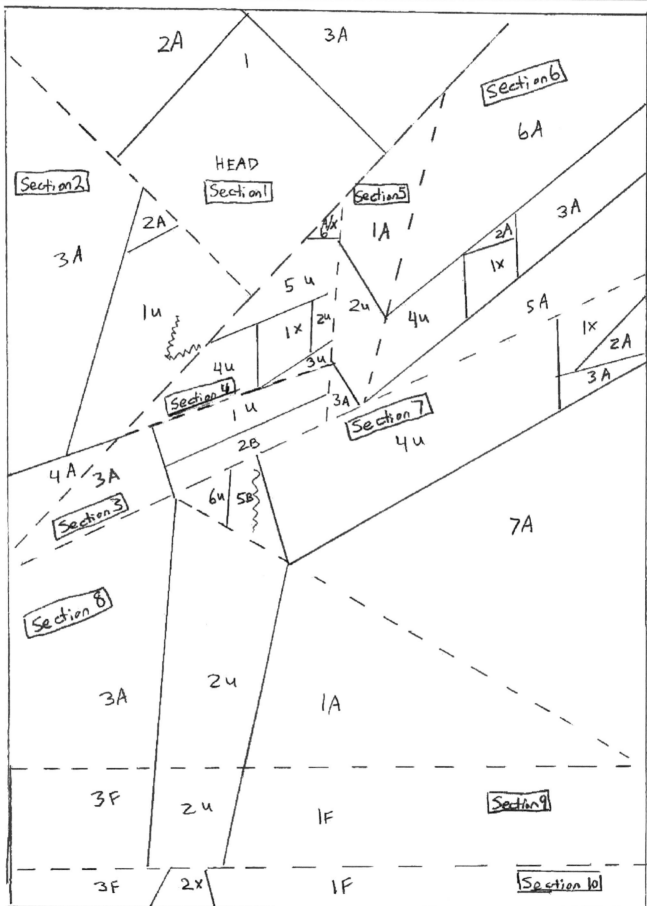

2A

3A

Section 6

6A

Section 2

HEAD

Section 1

Section 5

1A

6x

2A

3A

2A

3A

1u

5u

2u

1x

2u

4u

5A

1x

2A

1x

4u

2u

3u

3A

Section 4

1u

3A

Section 7

4u

2B

4A 3A

Section 3

6u 5B

7A

Section 8

3A

2u

1A

3F

2u

1F

Section 9

14

3F

2x

1F

Section 10

Patterns of BLOCKS and HEADS with Assembly Instructions

Works with all HEADS

*M*ake HEAD, then piece section 1. Piece section 2; join to section 1. Piece sections 3 & 4; join. Piece section 5; join to 3 / 4. Piece section 6; join to 3/4/5. Join section 1 /2 to 3/4/5/6. Piece sections 7 & 8; join. Piece section 9; join to 7/8. Join sections 1/2/3/4/5/6 to 7/8/9. Piece section 10, and then join to 1/2/3/4/5/6/7/8/9 to complete the BLOCK.

Pattern for BLOCK # 1, The Aggressive Position called Basic Front Kick

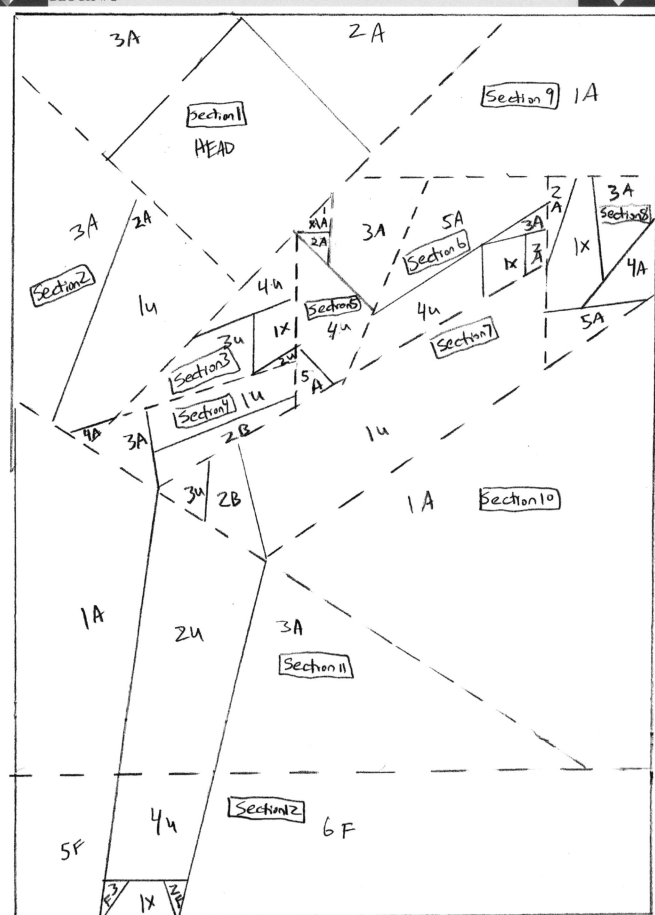

 All HEADS will work, but decide which style you will use, choosing either the Internal Chin or External Chin style HEAD, before beginning instructions, so that you will know which ones to follow.

Directions for Internal Chin style HEAD:
Make the HEAD, then piece section 1. Piece section 2; join. Piece sections 3 & 4 join. Piece section 5 (treat *X, *A, and 1 as one whole piece). Piece section 6; join to section 5. Join section 7 to 5/6. Piece section 8; join to 5/6/7. Join 9 to 5/6/7/8. Join section 3/4 to 5/6/7/8/9. Join 1/2 to 3/4/5/6/7/8/9. Piece section 10; join to 1/2/3/4/5/6/7/8/9. Piece section 11; join to 1/2/3/4/5/6/7/8/9/10. Piece section 12; join to 1/2/3/4/5/6/7/8/9/10/11 to complete the BLOCK.

Directions for when using an External Chin style HEAD:
Assemble the same as when using an Internal Chin, except when you piece section 5, join *X (chin) & *A (background) to form piece #1 of the section, then continue to finish the section.

Pattern for BLOCK # 2, The Aggressive Position called Basic Heel Kick

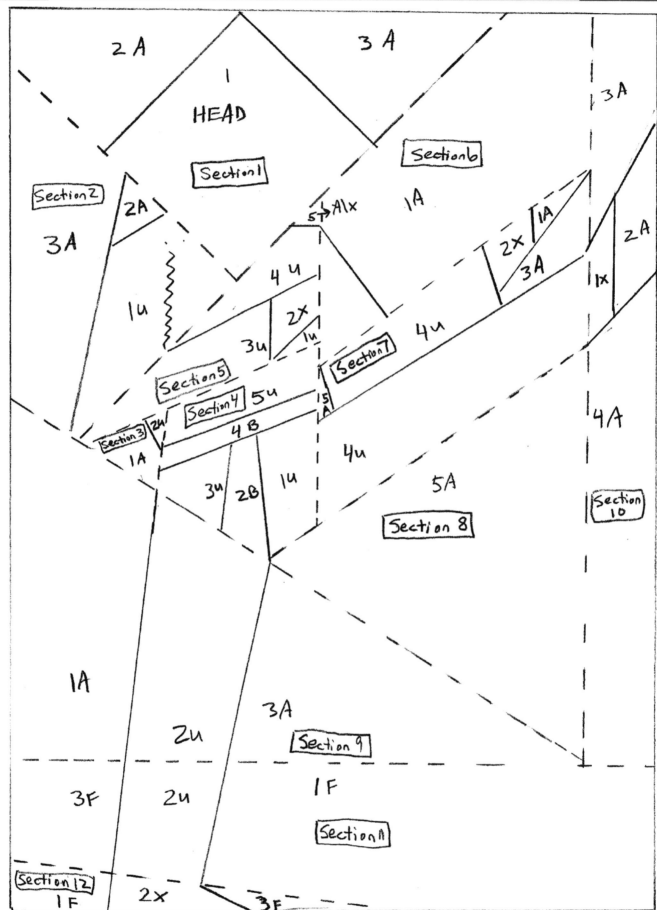

2 A

3 A

3A

1
HEAD

Section1

Section6

Section2

2A

3A

1A

5 A1x

2x 1A

3A

2A

1u

4 u

2X

1x

3u 1u

4u

Section5

Section7

4u

Section4 5u

Section3 2u

5 A

4A

1A

4 B

4u

3u 2B 1u

5A

Section 8

Section 10

1A

3A

2u

Section 9

3F 2u

1 F

SectionA

18

Section 12

1 F

2X

3F

*A*ll HEADS will work, though chin will be small if using external chin. Remember to color Piece # 5a/x in Section 5, either the background color "a" of the BLOCK or the color of a chin "x", depending on which HEAD is chosen.

Make HEAD, and then section 1. Piece section 2; join to section 1. Piece sections 3 & 4; join. Piece section 5; join to 3/4. Piece sections 6 & 7; join. Join 3/4/5 to 6/7. Join 1/2 to 3/4/5/6/7. Piece section 8; join to 1/2/3/4/5/6/7. Piece section 9 & 10; join. Join 1/2/3/4/5/6/7/8 to 9/10. Piece section 11; join to 1/2/3/4/5/6/7/8/9/10 to complete the BLOCK.

Pattern for BLOCK # 3, The Aggressive Position called Varied Heel Kick

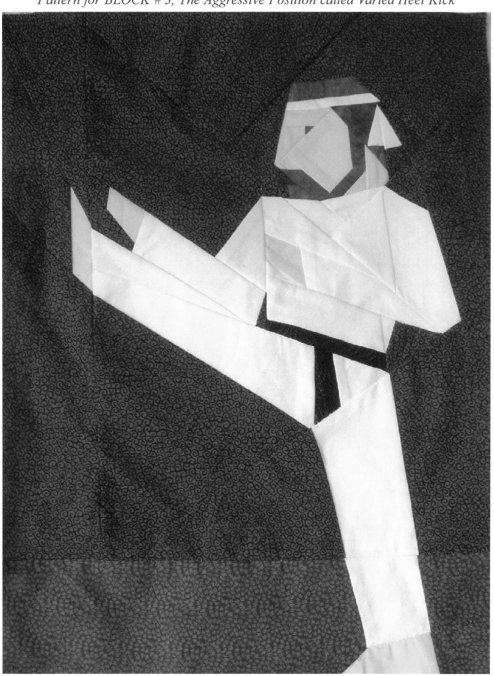

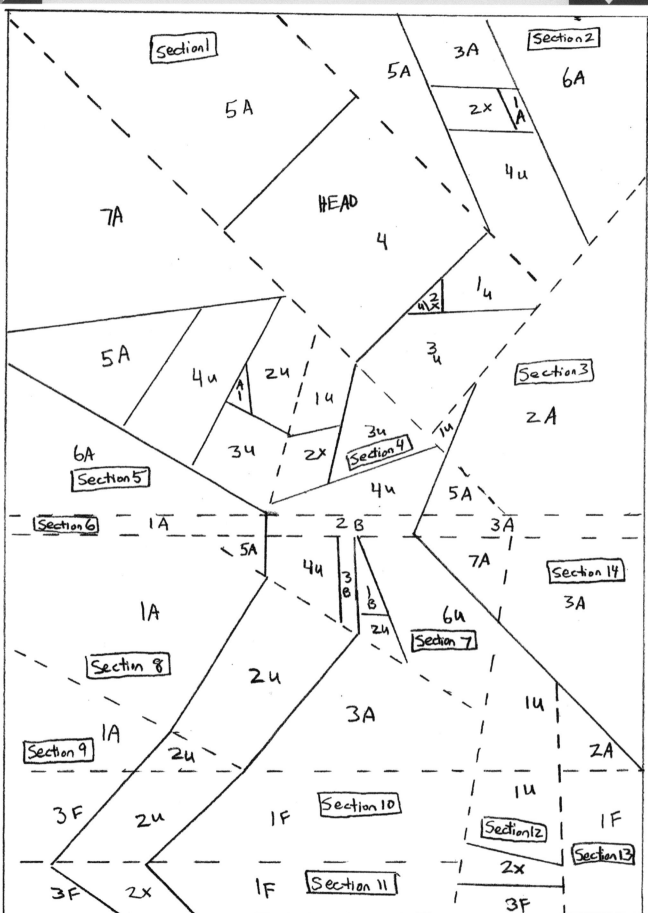

Section1

5A

5A

7A

5A

Section 2

3A

5A

6A

2x | 1 A

4u

HEAD

4

4 2 x

1 u

3 u

Section 3

2 A

4u | 2u

A 1

1 u

6A

Section 5

3u

2x

3u

Section 4

1u

4u

5A

3A

Section 6

1A

2 B

7A

Section 14

5A

4u

3 B | 1 B

6u

3A

1A

2u

Section 7

Section 8

2u

3A

1u

1A

Section 9

2u

2A

1u

3 F

2u

1F

Section 10

1F

Section 12

1F

Section 13

Section 9

2u

2x

1F

Section 11

2x

3F

20

3F

2x

3F

*A*ll HEADS will work, but decide which style you will use, either an internal chin HEAD box, or external chin HEAD box, before beginning the instructions, so you will know which one to follow.

Directions for External Chin:
Make the HEAD, then piece section 1. Piece section 2; join to section 1. Piece section 3; join to 1/2. Piece sections 4 & 5; join. Join 1/2/3 to 4/5. Piece section 6; join to 1/2/3/4/5. Piece section 7 & 8 & 9; join. Piece sections 10 & 11; join. Join 7/8/9 to 10/11. Piece sections 12 & 13; join. Piece section 14; join to 12/13. Join 7/8/9/10/11 to 12/13/14. Join 1/2/3/4/5/6 to 7/8/9/10/11/12/13/14 to complete the BLOCK.

Directions for Internal Chin:
Make pieces 1 & 2 & 3 in section 1 just 1 single piece, the color of the uniform, then continue with the directions above.

Pattern for BLOCK # 4, The Defensive Position called Rising Head Block

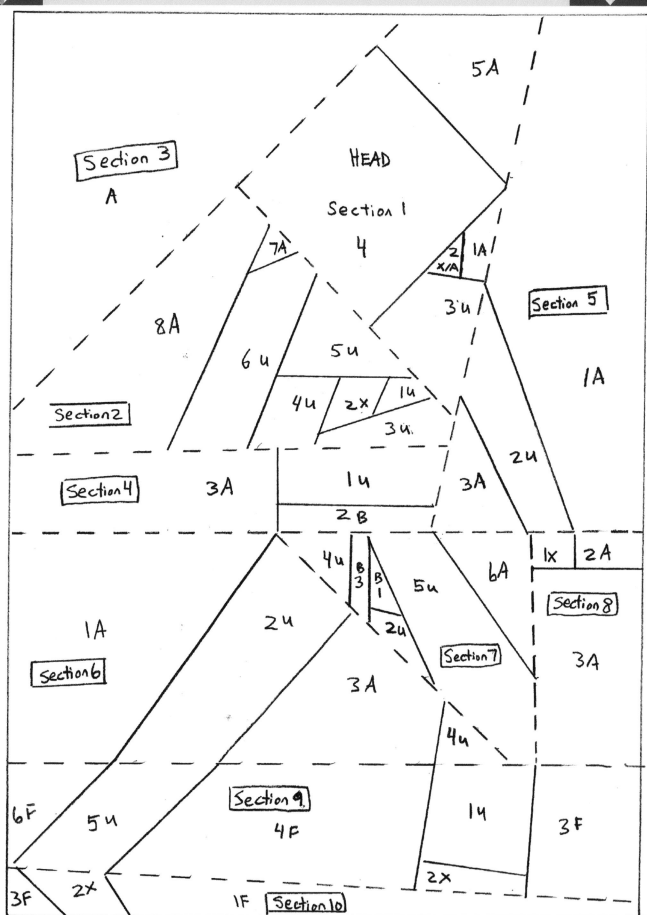

Section 3

A

HEAD

Section 1

4

5A

7A

2
X/A

1A

Section 5

3 u

8A

1A

6 u

5 u

4 u   2X   1 u

3 u

Section 2

2 u

Section 4   3A

1 u

3A

2 B

1 x   2 A

4 u   B
3   B
1   5 u

6A

Section 8

1A

Section 6

2 u

2 u

3 A

Section 7

3 A

4 u

6 F

5 u

Section 9

4 F

1 u

3 F

2 X

22   3 F   2 X

1 F   Section 10

External Chin

*M*ake the HEAD; then, in Section 1, join the pieces. Piece section 2; join to 1. Join section 3 to 1/2. Piece section 4; join to 1/2/3. Piece section 5; join to 1/2/3/4. Piece sections 6 & 7; join. Piece section 8; join to 6/7. Piece section 9; join to 6/7/8. Piece section 10; join to 6/7/8/9. Assemble 1/2/3/4/5 to 6/7/8/9/10 to complete the block.

Internal Chin

Follow the same directions above except in Section 1, make the Pieces 1 & 2, one single Piece of background fabric "A". Then continue on with piece # 3.

Pattern for BLOCK # 5, The Defensive Position called Down Block

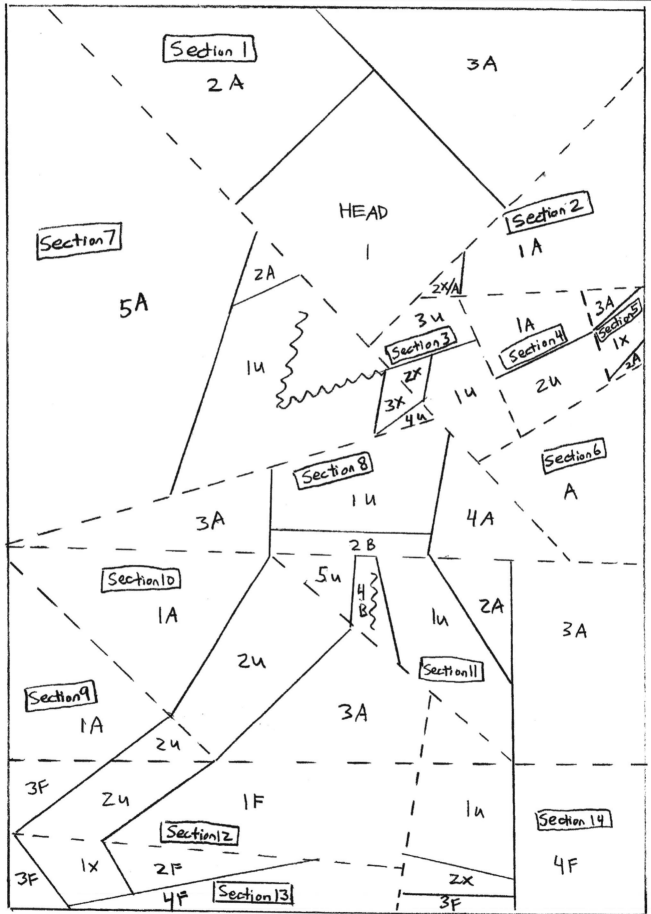

Section 1
2A

3A

HEAD
I

Section 2
1A

Section 7

2A

5A

2X/A

1u

3u

1A

3A

Section 5
1X

Section 3

Section 4

3A

2X

2u

1u

3X

4u

Section 6

A

Section 8
1u

3A

4A

2B

Section 10

5u

1A

4
B

1u

2A

3A

2u

Section 11

Section 9
1A

2u

3A

2u

3F

2u

1F

1u

Section 14

Section 12

4F

3F

1X

2F

2X

3F

4F

Section 13

24

*W*orks with all HEADS

*N*ote: If using external chin, use the #2 piece, in section #2 as the chin. If using an internal chin, treat section # 2 as 1 piece of the background fabric.

Make HEAD, then piece section 1. Piece sections 2 & 3 & 4 & 5 & 6; join. Join section 1 to 2/3/4/5/6. Piece sections 7 & 8; join. Join 1/2/3/4/5/6 to 7/8. Piece sections 9 & 10 & 11; join. Join 1/2/3/4/5/6/7/8 to 9/10/11. Piece sections 12 & 13; join. Piece section 14; join to 12/13. Join 1/2/3/4/5/6/7/8///9/10/11to 12/13/14 to complete the BLOCK.

Pattern for BLOCK # 6, The Defensive Position called Double Shuto

Pattern for HEAD # 1, A & B & C, External Chin, Single Section

Piece section 1 to complete the HEAD. Remember to add skin color to chin area of BLOCK selection.

A

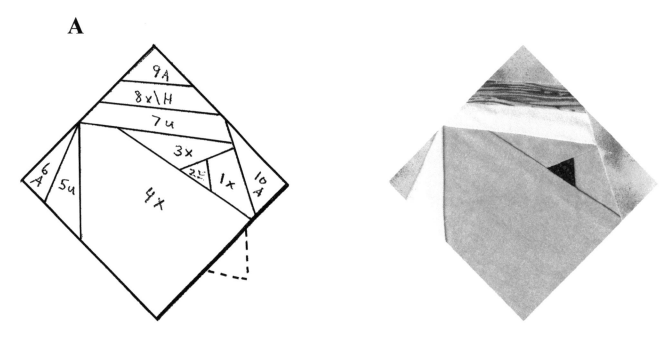

Pattern "A" using white color in eye area then adding a button

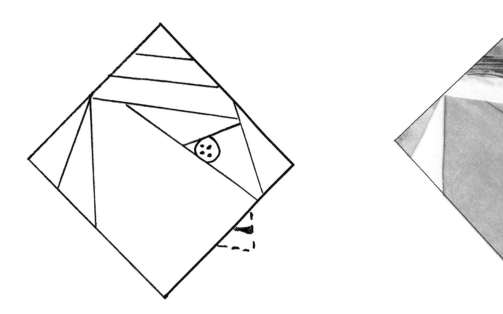

HEAD # 1

B

C

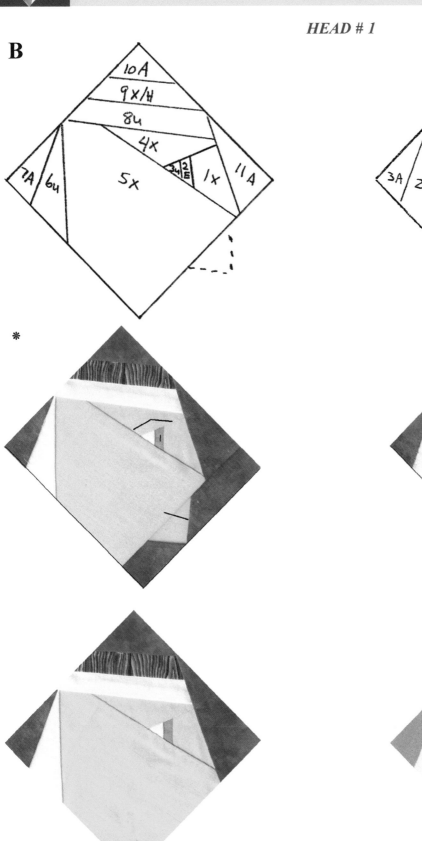

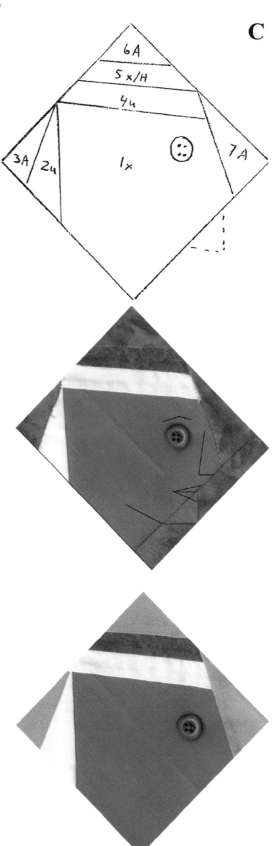

*

Pattern for HEAD # 2, External Defined Chin, Single Section, No Hair

*P*iece section 1 as indicated to complete the HEAD. Remember to add skin color to the chin area of the BLOCK selection.

Example shown as HEAD within BLOCK area.

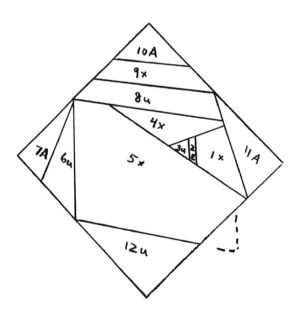

**Pattern for HEAD # 3, External Chin,
Single Section, Long Hair With No Bangs**

$\boldsymbol{P}$iece together the single section to complete the HEAD.   Remember to add skin colored fabric to the chin area of the BLOCK.

* Before beginning, refer to HEAD #1 for various selections of eye areas to choose from.

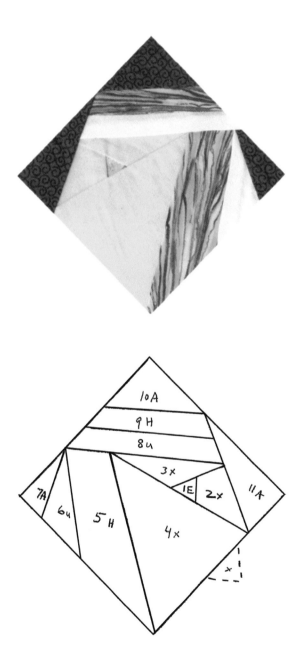

Pattern for HEAD # 4, External Chin,
Single Section, Long or Short Hair

*N*ote: Before beginning, chose between what type of eye and hair style you would prefer. To make a button eye: make pieces 1,2,3,4 one single piece of skin color "x". The instructions are applicable to each style. Piece this single section as indicated to complete the HEAD.

Note: Remember to piece the chin/mouth area into the body BLOCK pattern.

Suggestions: You may want the neck area to be the color of the skin or the color of the karate uniform. Also, in the eye area, an embroidery stitch could be used to create a nice eye, as well as for the lip area of the external chin.

See BLOCK #6 for an example.

Example below shows pieced eye with long hair without the chin, which will be added in the BLOCK pattern:

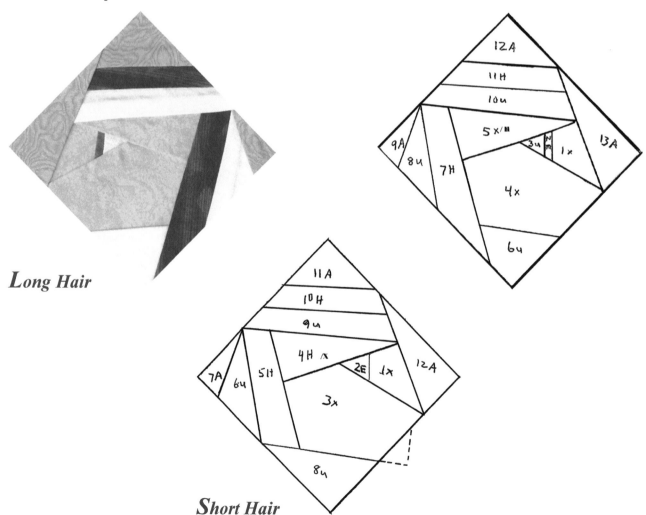

Long Hair

Short Hair

Pattern for HEAD # 5, Internal Chin,
Multiple Sections, Long Hair With Button Eyes

P*iece* sections 1 & 2 & 3; join. Join section 4 to 1/2/3 to complete piecing the HEAD.
Add eye and mouth if desired, using a button, embroidery, or permanent ink markers.

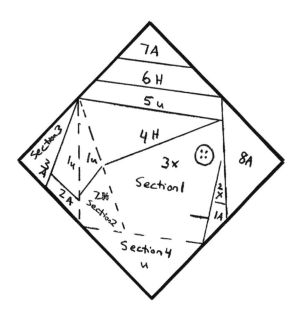

Pattern for HEAD # 6, Internal Chin,
Multiple Sections, Short Hair and Narrow Eyes

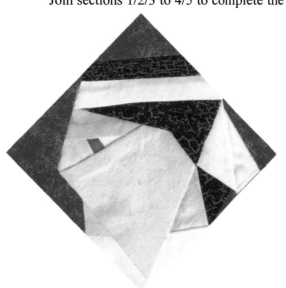 **P**iece sections 1 & 2; join. Piece section 3; join to 1/2 . Piece sections 4 & 5; join. Join sections 1/2/3 to 4/5 to complete the HEAD.

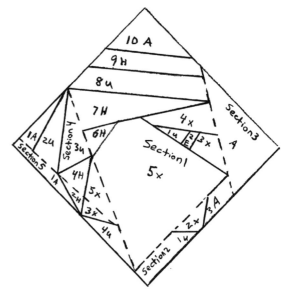

Pattern for HEAD # 7, Internal Chin,
Multiple Sections, Button Eye, Short Hair

 **P**iece sections 1 & 2; join. Piece section 3; join to 1/2. Piece section 4; join to 1/2/3. Join section 5 to 1/2/3/4 to complete piecing the HEAD. Add eye and mouth if desired, using a button, embroidery, or permanent ink markers.

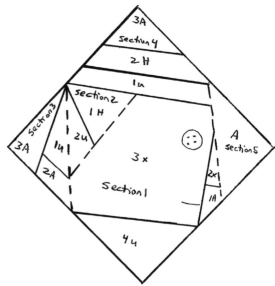

Pattern for HEAD # 8 A & B, Internal Chin, Multiple Sections, "A" Short Hair with Bangs and No Neck Showing, "B" Neck Showing and Altered Headpiece

*N*ote: The neck area in Section 2, can either be 1 piece of fabric using the karate uniform fabric color, or skin color in diagram "a". If you just want skin color in the center of section 2, use diagram "b". The karate uniform color will be for pieces 1 & 3, and the skin color in piece 2. The instructions that follow are applicable to either choice.

Piece sections 1 & 2; join. Piece section 3; join to 1/2 . Piece section 4; join to 1/2/3. Piece section 5; join to 1/2/3/4, to complete piecing the HEAD. Add an eye and mouth if needed or desired.

(B) Shows altered headpiece in section 3

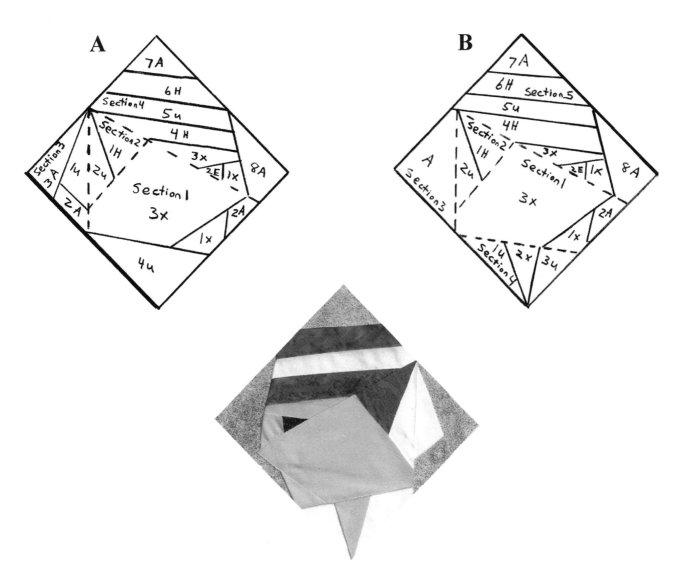

Pattern for HEAD # 9, Internal Chin, Long Hair with No Bangs

*P*iece sections 1 & 2 & 3 & 4; join. Piece section 5; join to 1/2/3/4 to complete the HEAD.

HEAD Example shown in BLOCK #9

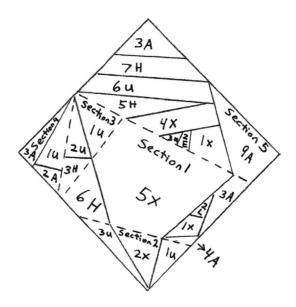

Pattern for HEAD # 10, Internal Chin, Long Hair with Bangs

*P*iece sections 1 & 2; join. Piece sections 3 & 4; join. Join sections 1/2 to 3/4. Piece section 5; join to 1/2/3/4 to complete the HEAD.

Note: Many small pieces in this HEAD

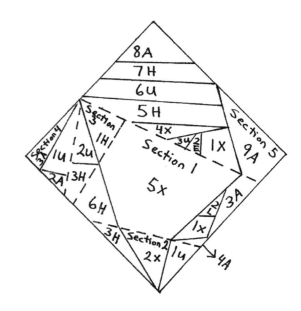

Pattern for HEAD # 11, Internal Chin,
Multiple Sections, Beard or Mustache

*N*ote: Piecing instructions are the same for HEAD #11 whether you chose the beard or mustache. Also, no eye pupil is included in the pattern, though it could be easily added if the pattern is enlarged enough. What is enough is a matter of personal taste. Personally, I would want the pattern enlarged at least 200% to justify the extra work for a tiny pupil which could be easily embroidered in. The same is true of lips or mouth definition. Embroider, draw, or quilt in the pupil in section 2, between pieces 1 & 2 , keeping the pieces together as the same section size.

Piece sections 1 & 2; join. Piece section 3; join to 1/2 . Piece section 4; join to 1/2/3. Piece section 5; join to 1/2/3/4. Join section 6 to 1/2/3/4/5. Piece section 7; join to 1/2/3/4/5/6 to complete the HEAD.

*M*ustache *E*xample

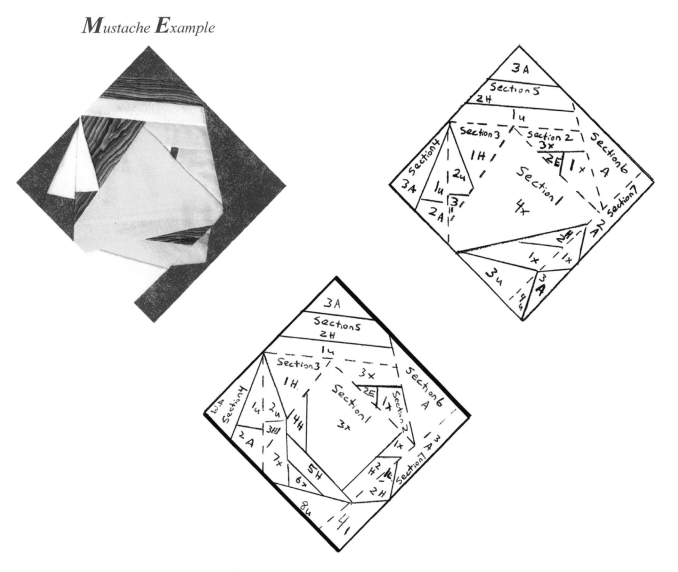

***B**eard Example shown in BLOCK #3*

Pattern for HEAD # 12, Internal Chin, Multiple Sections, Visible Neck, Goatee or Long Mustache

*P*iece sections 1& 2 & 3 & 4; join. Piece section 5; join to 1/2/3/4. Join section 6 to 1/2/3/4/5. Piece section 7; join to 1/2/3/4/5/6. Piece section 8; join to 1/2/3/4/5/6/7 to complete the HEAD.

Note: Section 3, Piece 1 color code could be "E" or "U". Section 7, is the mouth and goatee area. There Piece #1 fabric code is "H". Piece # 2 fabric code is "L"

*E*xample shown on BLOCK # 2 *The eye area
uses white fabric "U", with a button sewn on top.*

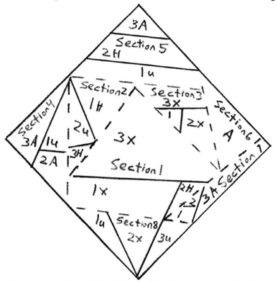

Pattern for HEAD # 13, Internal Chin, Multiple Sections, Short Hair

*P*iece sections 1 & 2 & 3 & 4 & 5; join. Join section 6 to 1/2/3/4/5 to complete the HEAD.

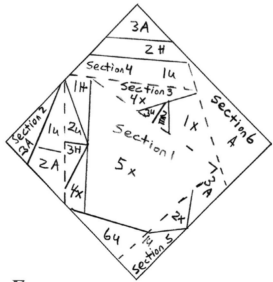

*E*xample shown in left figure of Example #1.

Finishing Touch

 *O*nce you have completed the BLOCKS used in the SAMPLE Pattern it is time to add the Ceiling, Floor and Walls. In this process you will be using larger pieces of freezer paper. If you have to combine freezer paper sheets together, put scotch tape on the non-shiny side.

Sampler Quilt Piecing Instructions
(See Action Karate Sample Pattern)

Put BLOCK #1 & #2 together. Add Sections 3 & 4. Piece and join Section 5 to the left side of the Block. Piece and join Section 6 to the right side of the Block. Now you have the top section of the quilt ready. Remove all of the freezer paper, by carefully tearing it off. You can now move on to basting.

Basting

Basting is temporarily securing the three layers of a quilt together, before the actual quilting is begun. The three layers are the Top, Batting, and Backing. Some people use safety pins to baste, and some use thread. When you have completed quilting, the basting stitches or pins will be removed. When you are quilting, the basting will help to prevent overlapping and buckling of fabric. To prepare for basting, lay the backing for the quilt face down. Then lay the batting you will use on top of the backing. Next, the top of the quilt will be placed face up (no pun intended), on top of the padding. If using pins, begin placing from the center of the quilt and working your way to the edges, spacing them no more than four inches apart. If using thread, take a long needle with a long piece of thread through it, and straight stitch the three layers together. Begin in the center area of the quilt and work out to the sides. Baste horizontally and vertically. No knotting needs to be done with the thread as you will want it to be easily removed.

*Note: Battings can be thick or thin. Years ago summer quilts were made with no batting at all. Select the type that is suitable for you.

Quilting

Quilting is application of the permanent stitches that will be used to hold the layers of the quilt together. Beyond this practical purpose, quilting can also add texture, embellishments, and details to a quilt. Remember to use good quality thread, as with all the work you do, you want it to last. Quilting by machine or by hand is a personal choice. Either way you will have to temporarily draw your quilting pattern onto the quilt top. Use quilters chalk pencil or temporary markers to place your quilt pattern onto the quilt. If you are quilting by hand, you will need to use a quilters hoop to hold your quilt while you are working. I use a small round wooden hoop, which is easy to take on an airplane or in a car. I also use a finger protector when quilting by hand.

A good quality stitch should be small and even. The fabric color may match the area you are covering or compliment it. When hand quilting, begin by threading the quilting needle. Knot one end of it. Completely pull the needle through the top layer of the quilt where you will begin quilting, so that the knot will be hidden behind the fabric. When you get to the end of the thread or your quilting area, backstitch over your last 3 or 4 stitches from the back of the quilt. Then forward stitch over them, before clipping your thread.

Binding

The binding is the final fabric that is run along the outside edge of the quilt. It connects the front of the quilt (top), the batting, and the back of the quilt (backing) together. You may select the color to either blend right in with the existing quilt and not be noticeable or go bold to add a picture frame effect.

There is also no set rule for how wide a binding should be. The size used in the Sample Quilt is 1/2" visible from the front. To keep this amount of binding as shown in Example #1, cut your strips to be 2-3/4". Then proceed with the Binding Process:

1.	For larger quilts requiring more than one binding strip to cover the peripheral edge of the quilt (Top / Batting / Backing), piece together the fabric strips using a bias seam. Trim excess corner. Press seam open. (See illustration)
2.	Press binding strips in half, lengthwise, back sides together.
3.	Mark the corners of the quilt 1/4" from the edge of the Top, for future reference.
4.	Front side of quilt facing up, beginning at the center, place binding with all raw edges even with the others. Pin. Sew through all layers using a 1/4" seam. Stop 1/4" from the end of the first corner, using your marking as a guide.
5.	Remove quilt from presser foot of sewing machine and prepare the folded mitered corner. (See illustration) Fold binding as shown, with the first fold at 45 degree angle, raw edge of binding extending straight with the second edge of quilt. Next, fold binding back down so that the top fold is even with the first edge of the quilt, and the raw edge of binding is even with the second edge. Slip quilt back under the presser foot and continue sewing, again stopping 1/4" from the end. Repeat folds and continue until you come to the starting point. Trim excess binding and flip under seam allowance, leaving a 1/4" overlap. Stitch to the end of overlap and backtrack to knot it.

6. With Top up, gently press binding toward the outside of quilt, carefully pressing into the corners. Turn the quilt over to the Backing and pin the binding down. This will cover the machine stitching lines. Fold corners to meet diagonally and pin in place. Begin stitching at the overlapped part of the binding, hand stitch the binding onto the Backing counter-clockwise using the Invisible Stitch. With this stitch you go down into the fabric and come up to the left of where you started. Then you proceed again by placing the needle back in from behind where you last come up, the coming up again to the left of your last stitch. This stitch is also used for appliqué, which is actually what you are doing as you do not want the needle to go through the Top of the quilt. You are just appliquéing the binding to the Backing.

Bias Seam Illustration

Making a Folded Mitered Corner Illustration

(in actual work, the edges of the quilt and binding match up to each other)

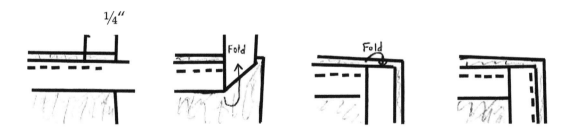

Project Size Reference

Knowing the dimensions of fabric pieces you may need to buy for a project may be helpful in your project strategy.

The average bolt of cotton fabric is 44" wide. So when you ask for 1/4 of a yard, it will be at least 9" x 44". A "fat" quarter yard is 18" x 22", 1/3 yard is 12" x 44", 1/2 yard is 18" x 44", and 3/4 yard is 27" x 44".

Quilts can be made into many items other than just for beds. Therefore, I find this handy guide very useful, and refer to it often. Upon putting it together, I was going to make a guide using inches and centimeters for the same bed, but found that the actual sizes of American beds and European beds differed. The American beds are listed in inches and the European beds are listed in centimeters.

Bed Sizes	USA Width/Length	European Width/Length
Baby Quilt	36" x 54"	
Afghan	54" x 72"	
Twin sized	54" x 90"	182cm x 228cm
Double sized	72" x 90"	225cm x 245cm
Queen sized	90" x 108"	245cm x 245cm
King sized	108" x 108"	275cm x 245cm

Table Sizes

On items such as table cloths, you may just want to use a quilt pattern as a border around the edge of the table. Also, keep the padding very thin or non-existent. The tablecloth sizes given are for a casual style. These sizes are approximate as table dimensions do vary though their height is relatively the same. What this means is that the drop over the side of the table will be no more than 10 to 12 inches. Often the drop over the edge of a casual table is 6 inches. A formal table drop is 16 to 24 inches. The distance to reach within 1/2 inch of the floor from the top of a table is approximately 28 to 29 inches.

Table Shape	Fits Table Size	Tablecloth Size	Amount Seated
Square	28" x 28" to 40" x 40"	52"x 52"	4
Rectangle	28" x 46" to 42"x 64"	52" x 70"	4 to 6
	36" x 56" to 42" x 64"	60" x 84"	6 to 8
	36" x 72" to 36" x 84"	60" x 104"	8 to 10
	36" x 90" to 36" x 96"	60" x 120"	10 to 12
Oval	28" x 46" to 42" x 54"	52" x 70"	4 to 6
	36" x 56" to 42" x 64"	60" x 84"	6 to 8
	42" x 72" to 42" x 84"	60" x 104"	8 to 10
	42" x 90" to 42" x 96"	60" x 120"	10 to 12
Circular	36" to 44" Diameter	60" Round	4
	44" to 60" Diameter	70" Round	4 to 6
	60" to 70" Diameter	90" Round	6 to 8
	17" to 19" Diameter	60" Round (to the floor)	Sofa End Table

Note: If you are making an octagon shaped tablecloth, use the circular shape for measurements

Pillow Sizes	Tablecloth Size
Pillow, large for sofa	24" x 24"
Pillow, small for sofa	12" x 12"
Bed Pillow Standard Size	28" x 20"
Bed Pillow King Size	34" x 18"

*S*quare Patch Reference

*S*hows the amounts of certain sized patches you can obtain from a certain amount of fabric.

Patch Size	1 Yard	½ Yard	¼ Yard
2"	357	178	89
2 1/2"	208	104	52
3"	154	77	38
3 1/2"	108	54	27
4"	80	40	20
4 1/2"	63	31	15
5"	56	28	14
5 1/2"	42	21	10
6" & 6 1/2"	30	15	7
7"	25	12	6
7 1/2" & 8"	20	10	5
8 1/2"	16	8	4
9" to 10 1/2"	11	5	0
11"	8	4	0
11 1/2" to 12 1/2"	5	2	0

*S*trips Available From 44" Wide Fabric

Strip Size	1 Yard	½ Yard
1 1/2"	23	11
2"	17	8
2 1/2"	13	7
3"	11	5
3 1/2"	10	5
4"	8	4
4 1/2"	7	3
5"	7	3
5 1/2"	6	3
6"	5	2
7"	5	2
8"	4	2

Bibliography

Jane Hall and Dixie Haywood. <u>Precision Pieced Quilts: using the foundation method</u>. Published in Radnor, PA 19089, by Chilton Book Co., 1992.

<u>Reader's Digest Crafts & Hobbies</u>. The Reader's Digest Association, Inc. Pleasantville, New York/ Montreal, 1979.

Dianne S. Hire. <u>Quilters Playtime: games with fabric</u>. Published in Paducah, KY 42002-3290, by American Quilter's Society, 1999.

<u>Quilting: patchwork & appliqué</u>. By the Editors of Sunset Books and Sunset Magazine, Lane Publishing Co. Menlo Park, CA94025, 1982

About the Author

*K*athy *A*zeez, a self taught quilter, has been designing and sewing quilts for 25 years. Like many other quilters, she loves quilting books, magazines, classes, and, of course, fabric.

For a number of years, Kathy, along with her son and daughter, pursued karate lessons for physical/mental coordination and activity. When her son became a black belt, she wanted to award him with a unique gift using this craft she loves. A search for karate patterns yielded nothing, so she decided to design them herself. The quilt she made won an award from the Third Annual National Arts Program in Cape May County, New Jersey.

Kathy is a member of the South Shore Stitchers Quilting Guild in Tuckahoe, New Jersey. When other members asked for the pattern, she adapted the pattern to make it flexible for a wide variety of applications.

Feel free to E-mail her with questions or comments:
KAZEEZQUILT@EARTHLINK.NET
www.actionkaratequilts.com

Printed in the United States
141821LV00002B